FOREVER PURRFECT JOURNAL

YOUR CAT'S STORY IN A JOURNAL

YOUR NAME: _____

CAT'S NAME: _____

Welcome to the Forever Purrfect Journal.

Writing Forever Purrfect is the inspiration for creating a keepsake journal for you.

The lined pages are an opportunity for you to write the story of your life with your beloved cat. There are no rules just what feels right for you. I've also included pages to record medications, vaccinations, special milestones, a paw-print page and a section for cherished photos.

Write from your perspective or from you cat's point of view. Whether its recounting the first time you crossed paths or their mischievous behaviour playing in the garden, that's entirely up to you.

To stimulate your creative notetaking, I've added prompts throughout the journal to help you write about the experiences of the day. The process of writing, can be cathartic and as you'll find, it can further deepen the bond you have with your cat. It's exactly how I felt when I penned Forever Purrfect. In time you'll have etched within these pages memories that will be forever perfect.

P.S. I welcome you to read Forever Purrfect, a heart warming story about an extraordinary cat named Sylvester. I've added quotes from Forever Purrfect throughout this journal as inspiration.

Enjoy writing!

Benito

MY CAT'S NAME: _____

D.O.B: AGE:
AGE WHEN ADOPTED:
GENDER: DESEXED:
BREED:
NOTABLE FEATURES
(KITTEN) WEIGHT   LB/KG   (YOUNG CAT) WEIGHT   LB/KG
(ADULT CAT) WEIGHT   LB/KG   (SENIOR CAT) WEIGHT   LB/KG
FUR TYPE:
BLOOD TYPE:
ALLERGIES:
ALLERGIES TO MEDICATION:
MICROCHIP:Y/N   REGISTRATION:Y/N
PERSONALITY TYPE:
FAVORITE FOODS:
FAVORITE DRINKS:
FAVORITE HOOMANS:
FAVORITE TOYS:
INDOOR OR OUTDOOR CAT:

VET DETAILS

VET'S NAME:
VETERINARY CLINIC:
ADDRESS:
PHONE:
EMAIL:
EMERGENCY CONTACT PERSON:
EMERGENCY NUMBER:
NOTES:

MEDICATION HISTORY

MEDICATION	REASON	DOSAGE	DATE	TIME

VACCINATION HISTORY

VACCINATION	REASON	DATE	FOLLOW UP

MEDICATION HISTORY

MEDICATION	REASON	DOSAGE	DATE	TIME

VACCINATION HISTORY

VACCINATION	REASON	DATE	FOLLOW UP

MILESTONES

Date: / /

Age

Date: / /

Age

Date: / /

Age

Date: / /

Age

Date: / /

Age

Date: / /

Age

Date: / /

Age

Write about your day with your cat ... Date:

What would your cat say about their day?   Date:

"I have a bed with a warm, comfy blanket in a room just for me."

Write about your day with your cat ...   Date:

What would your cat say about their day?   Date:

Write about your day with your cat ...   Date:

"Cats are the most enlightened of creatures, with their ability to be playful and curious with their surroundings."

What would your cat say about their day?   Date:

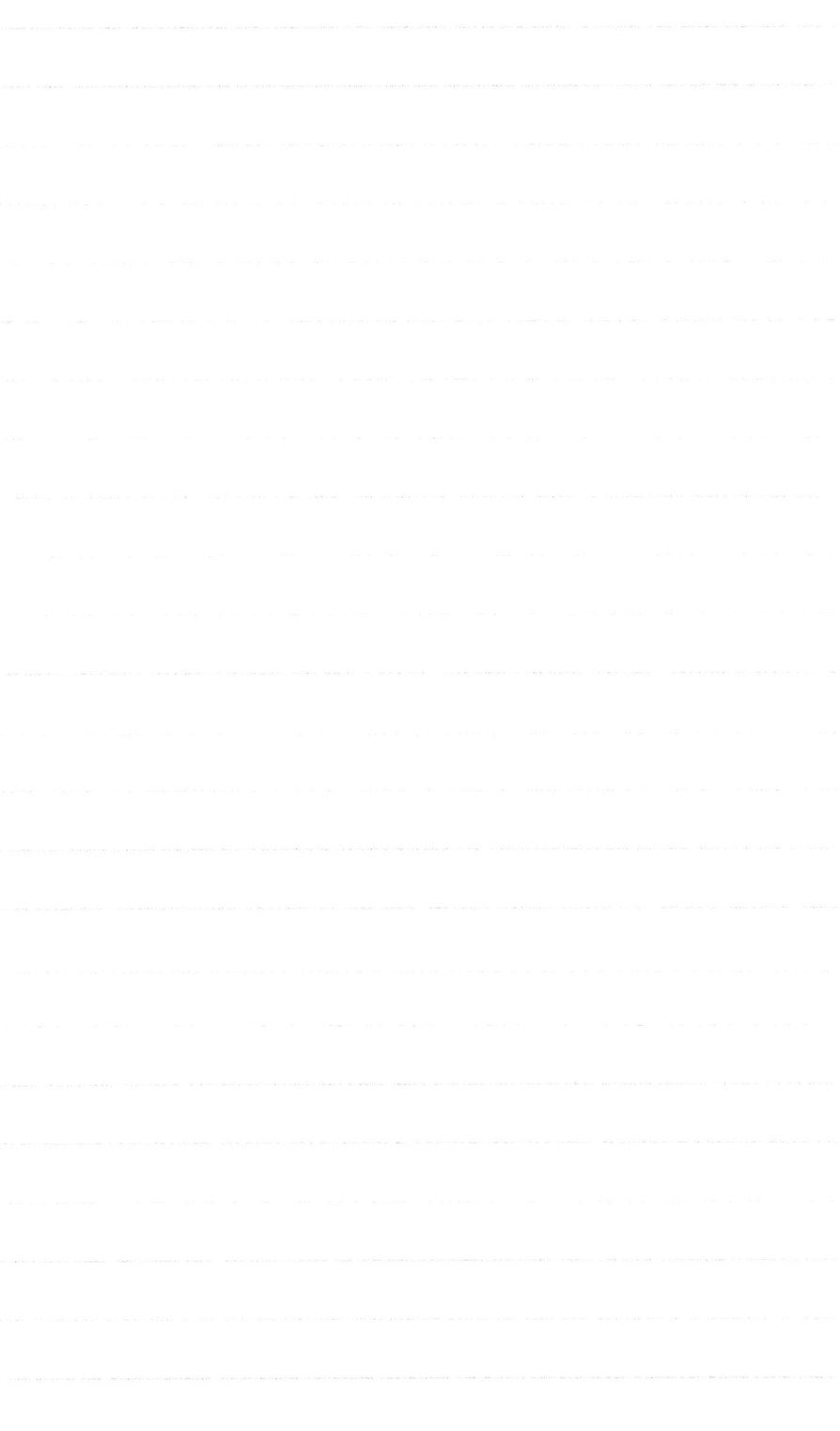

Write about your day with your cat ...   Date:

"I love food so much I could eat all day long. Every time I smell food wafting through the air, my attention instantly turns towards the kitchen."

What would your cat say about their day? Date:

"I have lived with several Zen Masters, all of them cats."
Eckhart Tolle

Write about your day with your cat ...   Date:

What would your cat say about their day?   Date:

Write about your day with your cat ...   Date:

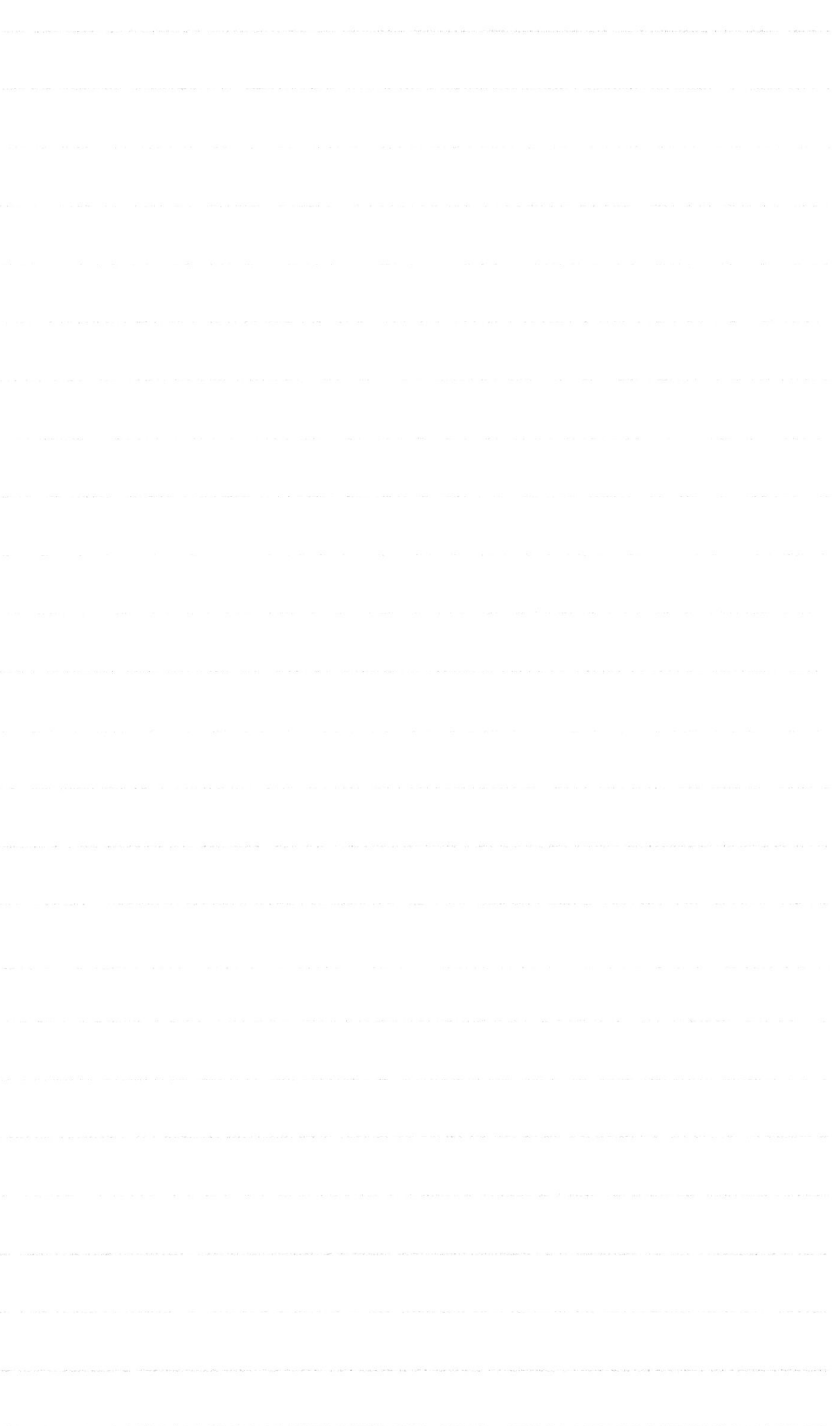

What would your cat say about their day?   Date:

Write about your day with your cat ...   Date:

"He was like a rock in the ocean that would sit and allow the ocean waves to sweep across it; he was just as resilient and unwavering."

What would your cat say about their day?   Date:

Write about your day with your cat ... Date:

What would your cat say about their day?   Date:

"Well, wasn't that a fun adventure?"

Write about your day with your cat ... Date:

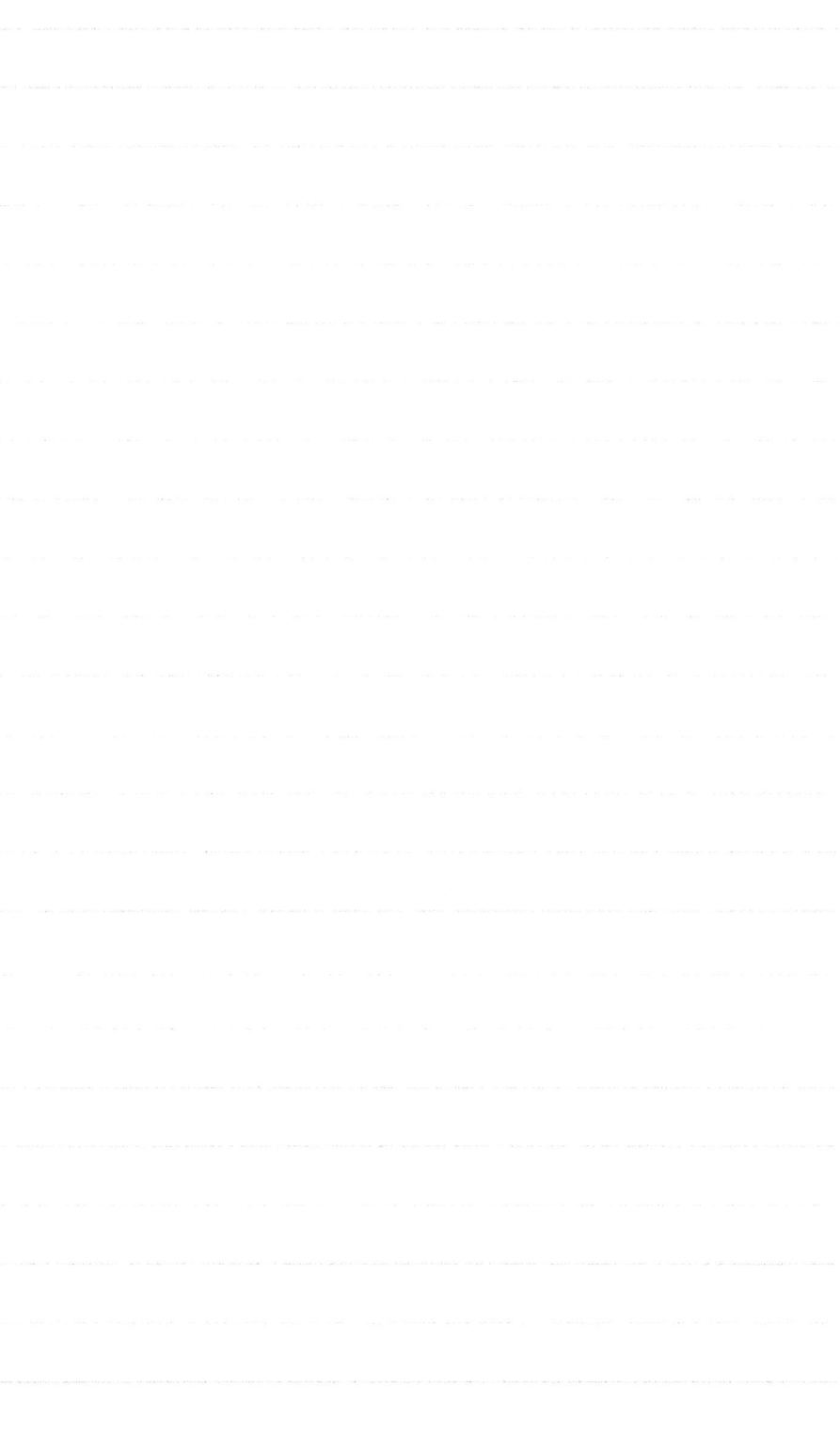

What would your cat say about their day?   Date:

Write about your day with your cat ...   Date:

"A fresh breeze blows in my direction. I lift my nose and smell the array of scents that travel with the wind. I smell home."

What would your cat say about their day?   Date:

Write about your day with your cat ...   Date:

What would your cat say about their day?   Date:

"In the waiting room, I notice a cat and a dog sitting with their human friends. The cat is attempting to sleep whilst the miniature white dog yaps away."

Write about your day with your cat ...   Date:

What would your cat say about their day?   Date:

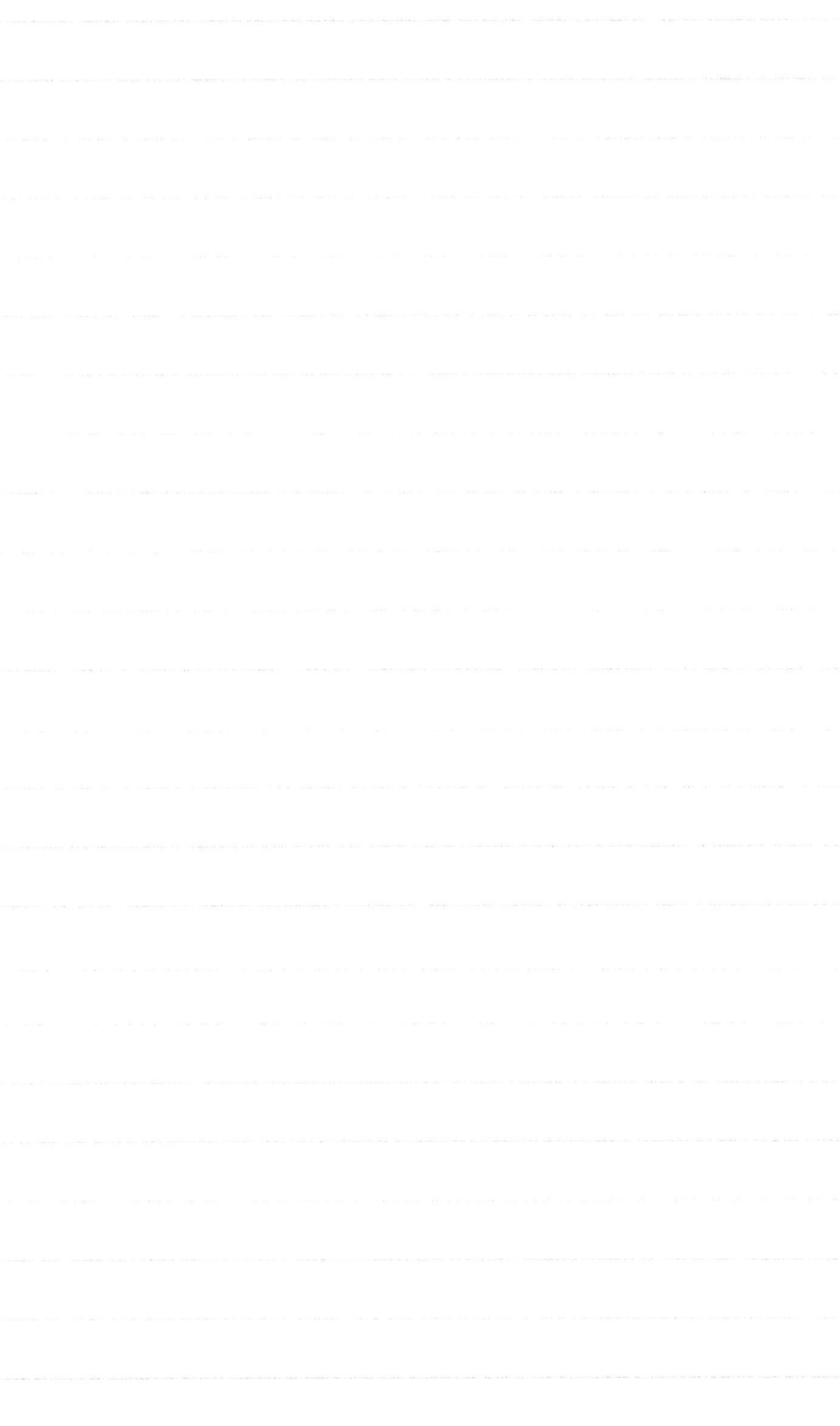

Write about your day with your cat ...   Date:

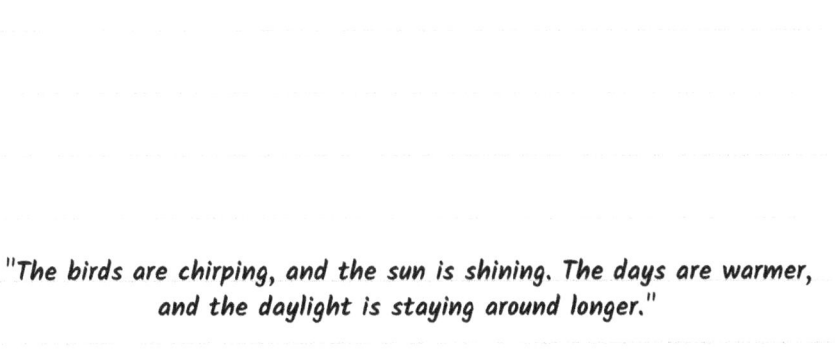

"The birds are chirping, and the sun is shining. The days are warmer, and the daylight is staying around longer."

What would your cat say about their day?   Date:

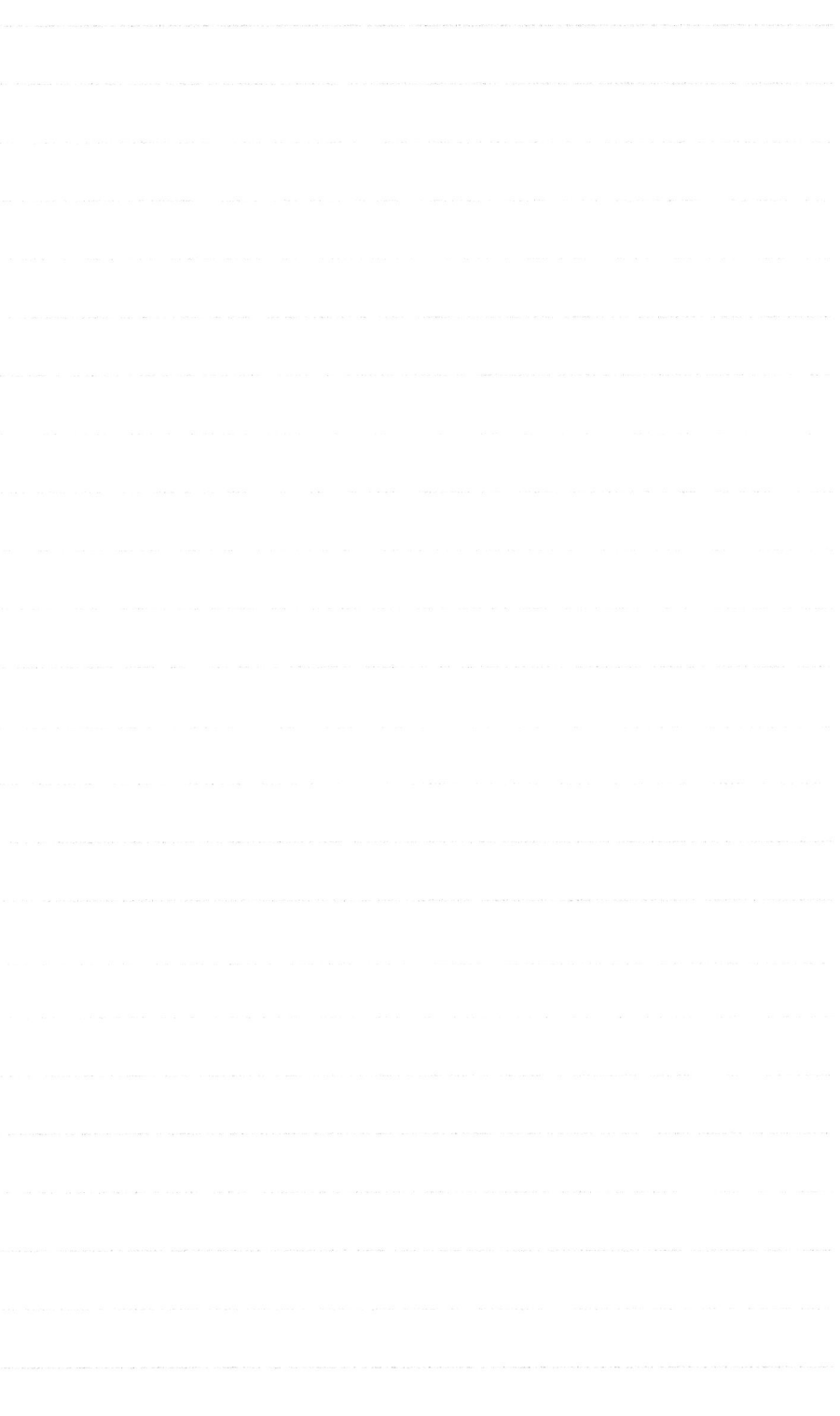

Write about your day with your cat ... Date:

What would your cat say about their day? Date:

"I look down at the ground and I see the ants marching once again. I fixate on one ant as it takes off in another direction. I wonder where he's going?"

PHOTO PAGE

PHOTO PAGE

PHOTO PAGE

PHOTO PAGE

PAW-PRINT PAGE

MY CAT _____ PAW-PRINTS*

kitten paw-print

young adult paw-print

adult cat paw-print

senior cat paw-print

* IT'S YOUR RESPONSIBILITY TO ENSURE YOUR CAT IS NOT STRESSED AND YOU USE ANIMAL SAFE PRINT AT ALL TIMES.

PAW-PRINT PAGE

MY CAT _____ PAW-PRINTS*

kitten paw-print

young adult paw-print

adult cat paw-print

senior cat paw-print

* IT'S YOUR RESPONSIBILITY TO ENSURE YOUR CAT IS NOT STRESSED AND YOU USE ANIMAL SAFE PRINT AT ALL TIMES.

Write about your day with your cat ...   Date:

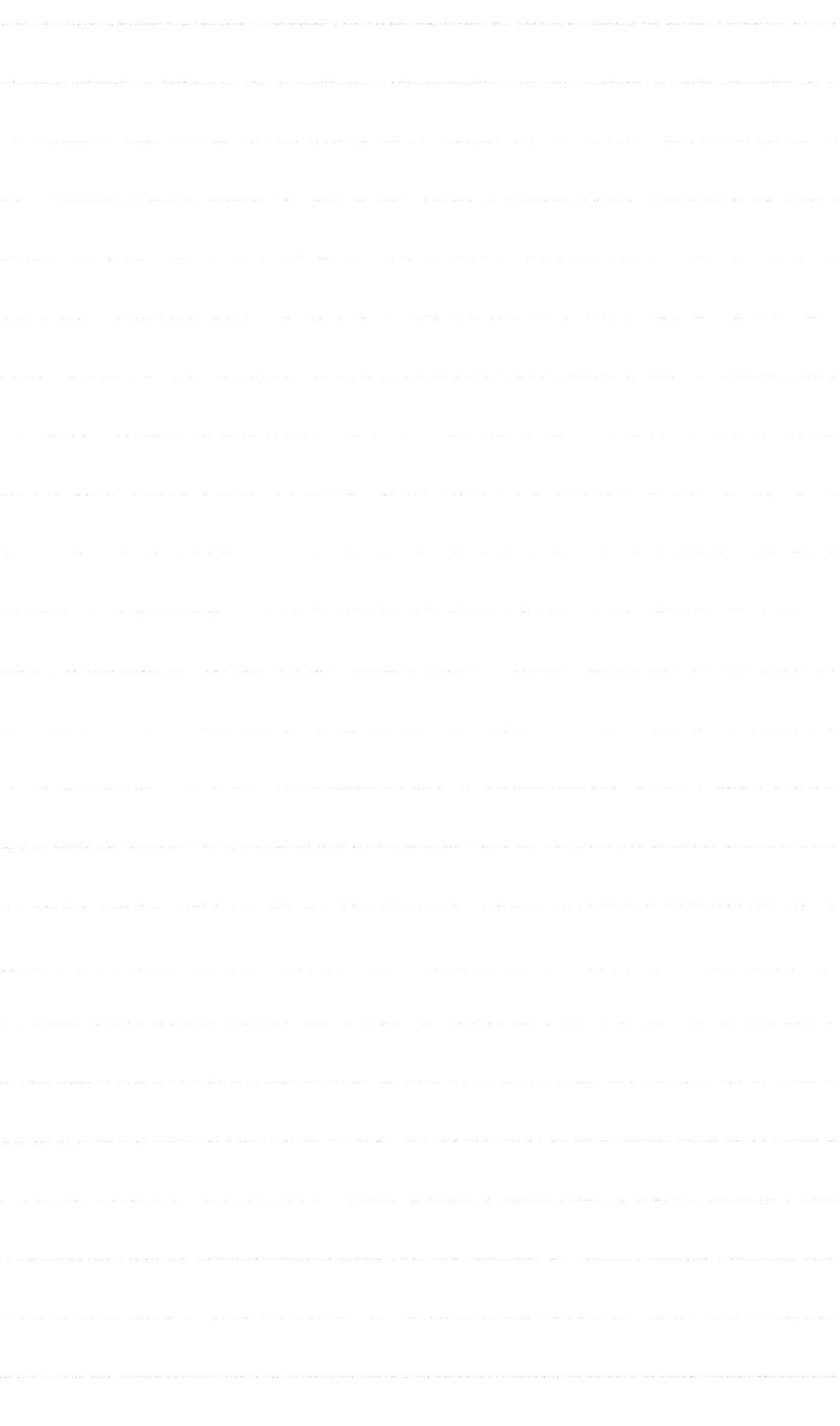

What would your cat say about their day?   Date:

Write about your day with your cat ...   **Date:**

"I take a step back, my eyes transfixed on the pieces of meat that tumble out of the tin and into my bowl."

What would your cat say about their day?   Date:

Write about your day with your cat ...   Date:

What would your cat say about their day?   Date:

"I notice a tree has been assembled in the lounge room. I like this tree because there are sparkling objects that hang off its branches."

Write about your day with your cat ...   Date:

What would your cat say about their day?   Date:

Write about your day with your cat ...   Date:

"It's a cat's obsession to be clean. It's a natural part of being a cat."

What would your cat say about their day?   Date:

Write about your day with your cat ...   Date:

What would your cat say about their day?   Date:

Write about your day with your cat ...   Date:

"As I peer outside, I witness the leaves dancing in the air as they dismount from their branches, landing softly on the brown dirt that surrounds the base of the tree."

What would your cat say about their day?   Date:

Write about your day with your cat ...   **Date:**

What would your cat say about their day?   Date:

"The most blissful part of my day is early evening when Mum sits down to relax in the lounge room. I jump on her lap where it's warm and comfortable."

Write about your day with your cat ...   Date:

What would your cat say about their day?   Date:

Write about your day with your cat ...   Date:

"I dream I'm running in the garden. I'm chasing a white butterfly as it attempts to fly away from me. I see a daffodil. It's bright yellow and smells wonderful."

What would your cat say about their day?   Date:

Write about your day with your cat ...   Date:

What would your cat say about their day?   Date:

"Time is fleeting, I think back to when I was a kitten, full of vitality and mischief. I'd race up and down the stairs and around the house. Nothing could catch me."

Write about your day with your cat ...   Date:

What would your cat say about their day?   Date:

Write about your day with your cat ...   Date:

"I look up at the fluorescent light; there's a fly buzzing and seeking attention. The animals and insects in this place want to be heard. I just want to get out of here and go home."

What would your cat say about their day?   Date:

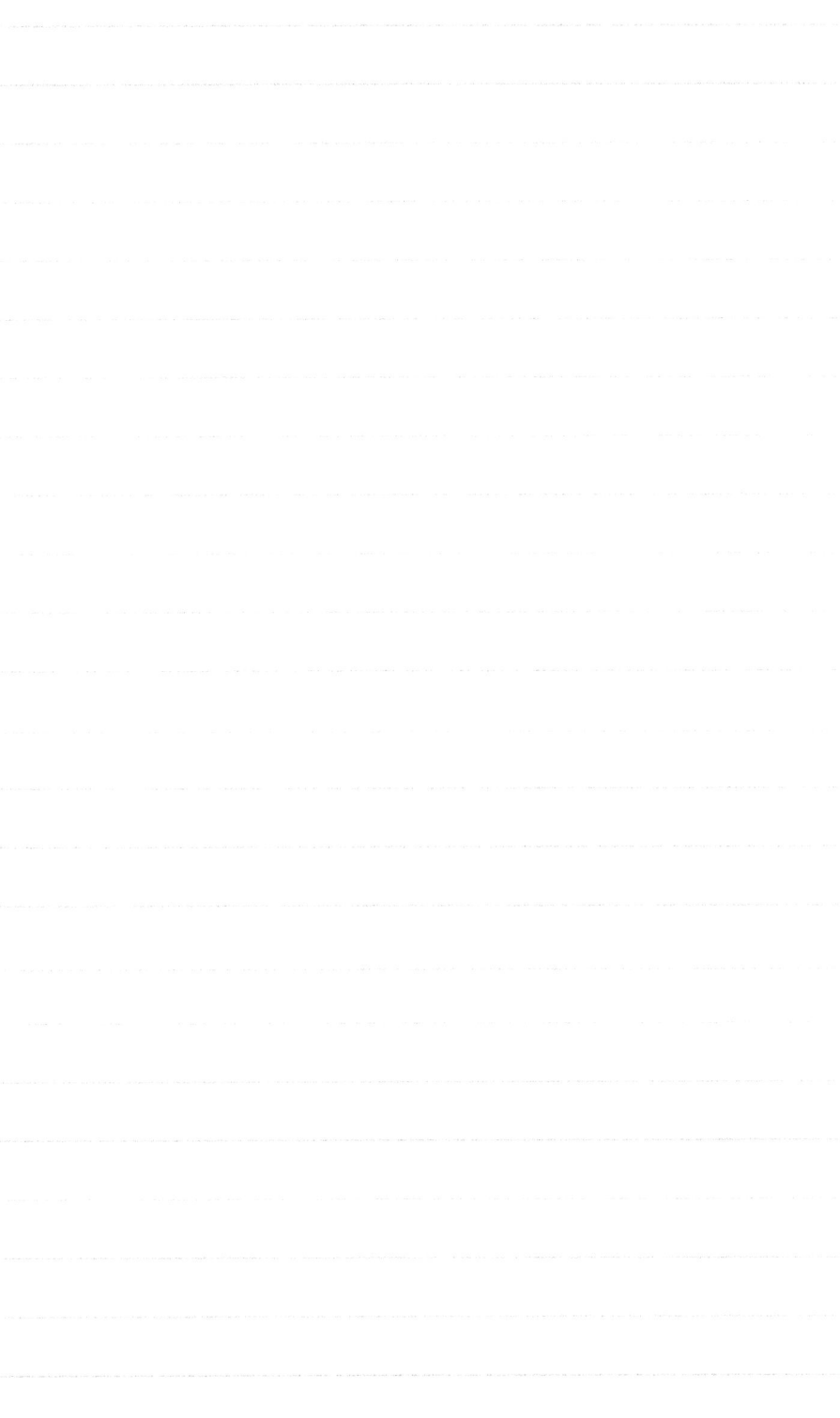

Write about your day with your cat ...   Date:

What would your cat say about their day?   Date:

"Animals are your best friends and they'll always be loyal to you."

Write about your day with your cat ...   Date:

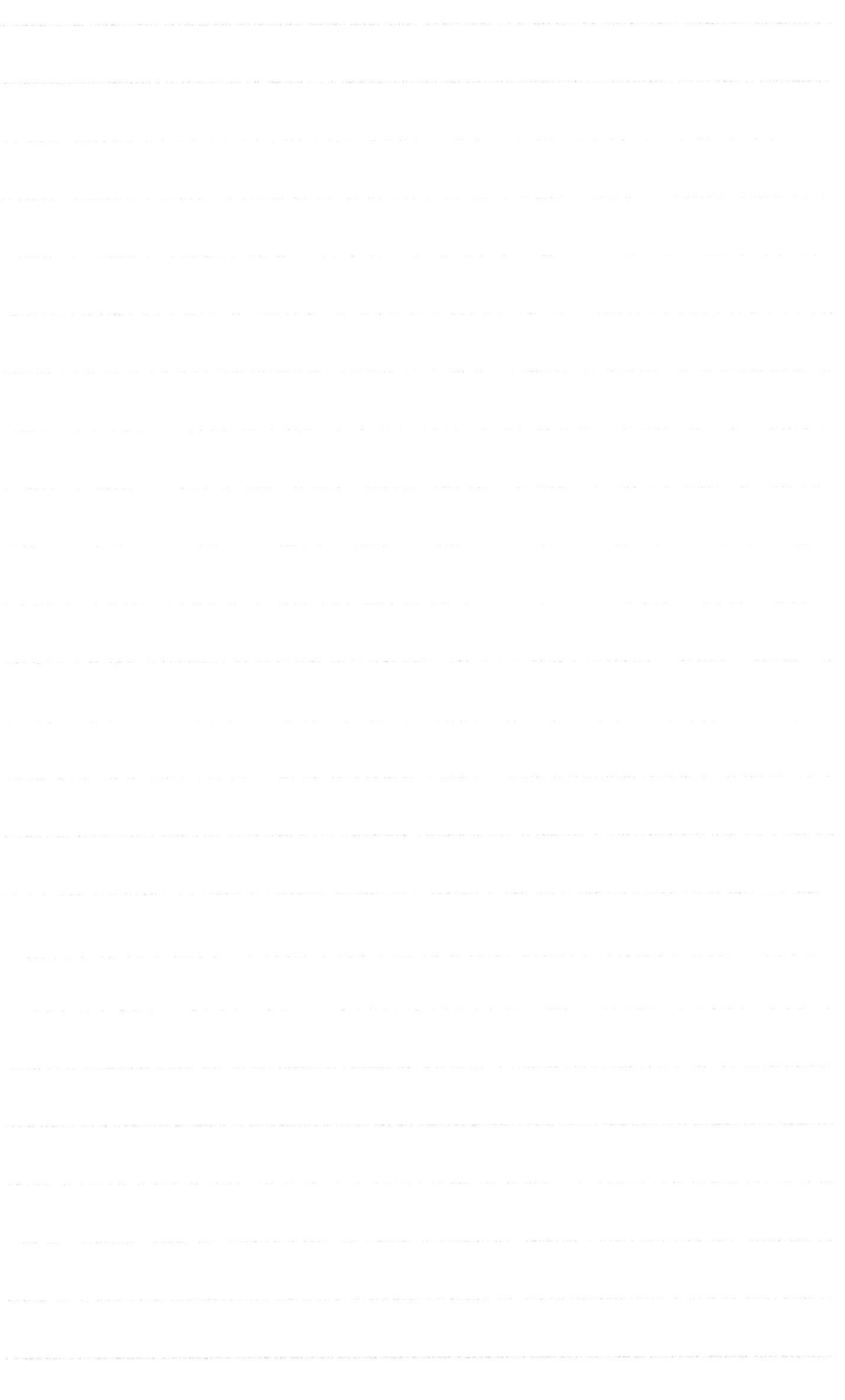

What would your cat say about their day?   Date:

Write about your day with your cat ...   Date:

What would your cat say about their day?   Date:

"Sometimes a very special cat enters our lives...
their presence changes our hearts forever.
And we can call ourselves blessed for having known them."
Unknown

www.ingramcontent.com/pod-product-compliance
Lightning Source LLC
Chambersburg PA
CBHW051538010526
44107CB00064B/2774